SHORT TERM RENTAL SUCCESS STORIES FROM THE EDGE

Volume 4

**BEAT THE REGULATIONS
2019 EDITION**

M2 Asset Publishing, Inc.
Av. Mutualismo 1321
Independencia 22055 Tijuana, B.C. Mexico

All rights reserved. No part of this book may be reproduced, stored in a retrieval system or transmitted in any form or by any means - electronic or mechanical, photocopying, recording, or any other - except for brief quotations in printed reviews, without prior permission from the publisher. Success Stories from the Edge (series and concepts), T.E.R.M. ®2008 and their Logo and Marks are Trademarks of Matt Malouf.

Although the author, co-authors, interviewees and publisher have made every effort to ensure the accuracy and completeness of information contained in this book, we assume no responsibility for errors, inaccuracies, omissions, or any inconsistency herein. The information in this book is sold without warranty, either express or implied.

ISBN: 9781075196188
2019 Edition
Publication Date: JUNE 2019
Version 1 © Copyright 2019 - M2 Asset Publishing, Inc.

To my beautiful, loving and supportive spouse Gladys, whose support and strength inspire me every day. To my kids who make life meaningful and worth living, thank you Andrew, Edward, Roxxane, Cally, Elon. Also, an extended thank you to the rest of my family and friends whose support and encouragement are appreciated everyday even if that list is too long to mention here, you know who you are. Love you guys (and gals).

Introduction

Welcome back to Short Term Success Stories from the Edge volume 4: Beat the Regulations! More and more, Rules and regulations, taxes and legislations, oh my. This maze seems to get bigger, more convoluted and crazier every day, especially in the short-term rental space. So many entrepreneurs experiencing so many growing pains, issues and frustrations with this. Everyday there are more and more articles about the troubles and issues being thrown at would be real estate entrepreneurs looking to enter or expand in the short-term rental space. Quite honestly some of the best stories I heard from people were operating their short-term rental business "illegally" and I put that in quotes for a reason, it really depends on how you interpret the laws in some areas and down the rabbit hole we go.

So, with this convoluted and complicated hot button topic, how can we share the most stories in an educational, informative and sometimes entertaining way to make the biggest impact? Especially since the best stories in this space came from entrepreneurs who, at the end of the day, decided not to share publicly the specifics (and generalities) of their stories. We did a mid-project pivot and interviewed many people within the regulation space and a few government officials to get their "unofficial" take the short-term rental industry and the implications of too many or too few regulations. We then compiled their "stories" together into topics to share with you some ideas how to turbocharge your success.

The first half of this book will explore some of the main questions and concerns regarding rules and regulations in the short-term rental industry, why they are needed and how we, as entrepreneurs, can use them to be ultra-successful in our given niche. The second half of the book will feature a few case studies around the world of how varying regulations work to give you an idea how to be successful no matter where you are and how hostile the conditions might be, I hope you enjoy and many thinks to all who participated in interviews informally and declined to be officially part of this project, your help is greatly appreciated!

No matter what external forces you face in your market, you can and will be successful!

Matt Malouf

Contents

Introduction iii

Overview of Regulations 1

Why do cities want to regulate short term rentals? 7

How can an Airbnb entrepreneur navigate increased
regulations and still be successful? 13

How can an Airbnb entrepreneur partner with a real
estate agent to adapt to regulations? 19

How can a real estate agent help with my Airbnb listing? 23

Municipalities to clearly define regulations 25

What can municipalities do to get hosts to comply with regulations? 31

Airbnb Regulations in Los Angeles, CA 41

Airbnb Regulations in Paris, France 47

Airbnb Regulations in Toronto, Canada 53

Airbnb Regulations in Australia 60

Airbnb Regulations in Israel 68

About the Author 74

Afterward 76

Overview of Regulations

Rules and regulations in the short-term rental industry.

Introduction

The concept is fun!

The concept of Airbnb and other short-term rentals is genius: Book a space in someone's home for far less than a conventional hotel stay.

Users of these short-term rental spaces can usually expect spacious accommodation in residential neighborhoods, lots of amenities and flexibility in arrival or departure times.

It is also a fun way to meet people and learn about the local culture.

Entrepreneurs are cashing in on the trend.

It is no wonder that more and more entrepreneurs are turning to the short-term rental industry as a way of increasing their income.

Overview of rules and regulations

This piece serves as a short overview of the rules and regulations of Airbnb, VRBO and other short-term rental agencies.

Legal restrictions on short-term rentals are not uniform across the spectrum and can be confusing.

There are regulations as to what type of home you have, where it is located and the length of the rental period.

Airbnb's general list

Airbnb provides a general list of do's on their website.

It outlines first what they expect their hosts to supply in terms of emergencies (a list of emergency numbers, a first aid kit, and fire prevention measures).

They also ask hosts to be mindful of their guest's privacy, adhere to occupancy laws, make their establishment child-proof and identify slip-and-fall hazards.

A host must remind their guests to stick to building- and parking rules, and alert them to regulations as to smoking, pets, and noise.

Local regulations

Local regulations are touched on briefly.

Taxes

Hosts are reminded that local taxes and business license requirements that may apply to them.

This can include hotel- or transient occupancy taxes, sales tax, value added tax (VAT), Goods and Services Tax (GST) or income tax.

Registrations and permits

It is the responsibility of individual hosts to look up if they need a permit to start renting out their property. There might be zoning, safety- or health regulations that must be adhered to.

There is more than meets the eye

However, there are a lot more to it. Users that enter the short-term rental industry for the first time could be lulled into a false feeling of security by the general terms on the websites of Airbnb and other short-term rental agencies. It can be quite complicated to start following all of the rules.

Municipal restrictions

It is a minefield!

Municipalities in different cities and counties have different legal restrictions on short term rentals.

A rental owner who does not live in the same city as his rental might find that he needs to do some homework on the topic.

New York, New York

In New York City, for example, local rules say that an apartment within an apartment building must be used for 'permanent' residential purposes. It is illegal to rent out your whole apartment to someone if the stay is for less than 30 days as the property must be occupied by the same persons or family for 30 (or more) successive days.

There is, however, an exception: you may rent out a room in your apartment if you are also staying there and if the guest can have access to all parts of the studio.

On the other hand, in some cities such as Palm Desert and St. Helena in California, short term rentals of up to 27 days are allowed provided that the owner has an annual permit and pays a special occupancy tax.

Zoning laws

In other cities, zoning laws limit what you can and cannot do. For example, in San Luis, Obispo County, rentals cannot be too near to each other. Some counties limit the number of occupants to an apartment.

Not enforced

Municipal restrictions on short term rentals are not regularly enforced. Most municipalities don't have the human resources to follow up on all rentals in their counties.

Usually, they are unaware that there even **is** a short-term renting going on! It is only when there are problems, and the neighbors are complaining that a municipality will investigate.

Familiarize yourself

However, it is best to familiarize yourself on the rules and regulations on short term rentals in your area.

Violations can be met with hefty fines. Some cities and counties that require licenses and taxes are getting serious about it, and municipal laws are increasingly designed to regulate the industry. It is better to be safe than sorry.

An online search about laws and restrictions in the area where your property is situated should give you a good idea of what you should do to make your rental legal.

A real estate attorney that specialized in landlord and tenant issues should also be able to help if you are struggling to get information.

Legal restrictions on Condos

Condos and other planned developments usually have bylaws that may restrict short term rentals or bar them entirely.

The best policy should be first to ask permission from your homeowners' association before you rent out your condo. They will advise you as to the rules and regulations of your specific condominium complex.

A tenant yourself?

Tenants are usually not allowed to rent out their apartment on a short-term basis. Most leases contain a clause that prohibits sub-letting unless you can get the landlord's permission.

Should you want to make use of short-term rentals to supplement your income, you should first check your lease or talk to your landlord. Some landlords might be lenient and allow short term renting on certain conditions.

How to find out more

The Airbnb website

The Airbnb website summarizes the legal requirements of about 50 cities. Each of these 'city summaries' has links for more information. The first place to check for rules and regulations applicable to you, is here. (https://www.airbnb.com/help/article/1376/responsible-hosting-in-the-united-states)

Your local government

Should your city not be listed with the short-term rental agency itself, check your local government's website. The information should also be available at your local city hall, your city's zoning board or your local housing authority.

You can also check out http://www.stradvocacy.org/, a center created by short term rental agencies themselves.

Conclusion

The purpose of this article was to give a short overview of what short term rental hosts can expect when they start in terms of rules and regulations.

Unfortunately, it is impossible to give information to every owner out there as regulations are so diverse in different counties and cities. It is up to you to do the right thing and familiarize yourself on the conditions to be met in your rental's area.

It is no use to stick your head in the sand!

The rules are increasingly being enforced as the industry is developing and evolving.

In the long run, it will be beneficial to you to be up to date as to what rules are applicable in your situation.

Why do cities want to regulate short term rentals?

Introduction

Short term rentals are not contained to beach- and mountain towns anymore. Anyone with an attractive rental unit can now make money, thanks to the spectacular rise of Airbnb and other short-term rental sites.

As a result, cities, and counties are now increasingly confronted with the fact that the whole industry needs regulating.

Negative side-effects

Not everyone is happy with the innovation and the change from the traditional.

Some local citizens in Europe feel that their city centers are overcrowded and that they can't afford to live in their trendy neighborhoods anymore.

The rise of the short-term rental industry has also brought noise, trash-, traffic- and parking problems with it. It must be contained and managed.

Cities and counties must also consider the effect of short-term rentals on neighborhood character and affordable housing as a whole in the affected districts.

Owners of rental units must be aware of the tax requirements in their city and of how they can be tax-compliant. There is, as a result, a genuine need for home-sharing to be regulated.

Who is asking for regulations?

- Neighboring residents in popular short-term rental unit areas have the most to lose. They have to put up with an influx of tourists that often changes the whole character of the neighborhood.

It is not always negative, but it can be. It is understandable that these residents must be protected by some or other type of regulation.

- The traditional hotel industry was, before the short-term rental industry-boom, the leading provider of accommodation.

Home-sharing and private apartment rentals can operate at a fraction of the costs of the traditional industry and can offer accommodation at very affordable prices. It is almost impossible for the hotel industry to compete, so one can understand that they have a significant stake in the fact that proper regulations must be adhered to. **They** are subjected to rules, so the short-term rental industry must be, too.

Fines for non-compliance in the short-term rental industry can be substantial. In Miami Beach, Florida, first-time offender fines start at $20,000.

- Governments themselves see the need for regulations. Tax revenue is a significant advantage that can be gained from the short-term rental industry, and it can be used to make municipalities and cities even better for tourism.

See life through the eyes of a local

New, urban tourism that encompasses the short-term rental industry has travelers looking for authentic experiences 'off the beaten track.' They want to see how the locals live.

Out of the bubble

An increasing share of visitors, therefore, are moving away from doing the traditional 'touristy' things in 'tourist bubbles' and are finding accommodation in the historic centers of cities, originally not planned for tourism.

Regulation is needed because ...

The problem for cities and municipalities lies in increased nuisance complaints that may range from just a loud party to rancorous drunken behavior.

There are issues with hard-to-find parking, traffic in small streets and how waste is managed. Locals also have safety concerns with the invasion of strangers into formally quiet neighborhoods.

In an extreme example, residents in Barcelona, Spain, are reporting a progressive loss of local culture and cohesion in their neighborhoods due to short rental platforms.

Gentrification is also a problem.

Big commercial guys

Commercial investors are snapping up residential properties and turning them into short term rental units. In return, housing availability and affordability for locals become an issue. Research in New York has shown that property values have risen between 5-10% due to the doubling of Airbnb locations.

Although this might not be a problem for homeowners, other residents can no longer afford to pay rent. Over the longer term, a neighborhood can become unaffordable for local newcomers.

A city might want to regulate short term rentals aggressively if this is a massive problem for them.

Tax-compliance

The San Diego example

San Diego is a major tourist destination and families can now have an affordable holiday at the beach due to the rise of the short-term rental market.

In San Diego, each rental property must be registered and licensed. Occupancy tax is payable monthly, at 10.5%. The taxation of the short-term rental industry is a way that the city can recoup some of the 'losses' and spend more on better municipal facilities, roads, and services.

Hotel- and property managers have a typical high compliance rate to the regulations, but individual owners are not faring that well. This is because they are unfamiliar with the process and often unaware of their tax responsibilities.

There are still lots more educating that needs to be done. At the moment, lots of local governments are missing out on thousands of possible tax dollars due to a lack of proper regulation.

It is up to the city government.

It is up to each city to determine how they want their short-term rental landscape to look and instigate the appropriate regulatory framework to support this.

Each to his own

In effect, the *'why'* of regulation is a question that each city or county must answer for itself. They must base their decisions on facts and decide on what goals they have for control in the first place.

The size of the city, the established tourism industry and the concentration of Airbnb listings are all factors that should be kept in mind. Most cities feel that Airbnb and other platforms need to be regulated to balance the interest of visitors, residents and businesses.

In a city like San Diego, the influx of tourists might mean that better upkeep overall is necessary. It might also suggest that the available rental units for locals are less frequently available.

It is up to the city to know the trends and 'protect' the locals.

Conclusion

Strong growth forecasted

Travelers love the short-term rental industry, and it is expected that rising traveler demand will drive strong growth in this sector. Platforms such as Airbnb made the industry more accessible and gave the discerning traveler a variety of accommodation options.

However, ordinances are needed to eliminate party houses, keep residential neighborhoods residential and make sure that short-term rental hosts are paying their fair share in permit fees and taxes.

This is why cities have to regulate the industry.

Regulation issues are still in the early stages. But, industry experts mean that over the longer term, it will become more uniform and solutions will be found that will work in most communities.

How can an Airbnb entrepreneur navigate increased regulations and still be successful?

Short term rental industry

Introduction

In the first two articles of this series, we've overviewed rules and regulations within the short-term rental industry. We've also answered the question as to *why* cities and counties would want to regulate the industry.

In this article, we are zooming in on the Airbnb entrepreneur.

What does it all mean, to you? Is it possible to plot a course through all of the industry's regulations and still be successful?

You should know the legal considerations.

It is essential for the entrepreneur to understand the legal implications that come with the ownership of a short-term rental property. In this industry, where the rules are still fluent and ever-evolving, it is imperative to know what you are in for.

What is a short-term rental?

Do you think you know?

It might not be as straight-forward as you think. Most people will say a short-term rental is the rental of a room in your house or an apartment to a guest for a few days.

However, several key factors can influence the definition of a short-term rental unit.

- *The type of structure*

It depends on where you live. In Charleston, South Carolina, three categories or zone rules are in effect.

Under the first category, property in the old district can only be rented if listed on the National Register of Historic Places. The second category states that other homes in the rest of the peninsula are eligible for rental only if older than 50 years. Even so, only rooms can be rented.

Only in the city beyond the peninsula, short term rentals in any age home is allowed. The rationale here was to protect historic neighborhoods, but also to prevent commercial builders to build new properties specifically for short term rentals.

In Denver, Colorado, mobile homes and RV's are not allowed to be utilized as short-term rentals.

It is important to clearly understand the regulations in your area in terms of what structure counts as a short-term rental. It has an impact on **how** you rent out your space, but also what permits and licenses are needed.

- *May I take your coat?*

How long you are renting your place out for is also crucial in the quest for a short-term rental definition. In many cities, it is required that a guest is not allowed to stay for longer than 30 days. If such a person stays longer, it is no longer a short-term rental agreement, and you violate the rules.

- *No investors wanted*

Some cites do not allow the renting out of units where there is no primary resident. This is to stop commercial builders or investors from taking over a community and flood it with short-term rentals.

Legal restrictions

To be a successful Airbnb entrepreneur, you should also know what other restrictions regulate the industry.

- *Some cities prohibit short-term rentals in some way.* You should find out if there are any zoning restrictions in your area.

- Larger cities and popular tourist destinations may place limits on the *number of rental units* that are allowed to operate in a given area. In the French Quarter of New Orleans, for example, short term rentals are primarily banned, except for some small regions.

- 'Multiple Dwelling Laws' restrict short-term lets in some cities. It is unusually severe in New York City. Here, rentals in apartment buildings are only allowed if the permanent resident is present. The idea is to prevent nuisance to other residents in the building, but also to protect the hotel industry in the city.

To make sure you navigate effectively through all of the rules and regulations of short-term rentals, you should check the laws applicable in your rental area. Violations of the rules are met with stiff fines and will sure hamper you in your success.

The association rules of condos usually prohibit sub-letting and may limit your entrepreneurial endeavors. If you are a renter yourself, your landlord should approve your short-term rental aspirations.

Know what licenses and permits are required.

'Getting Started'

The Airbnb website and the websites of other short-term rental platforms are usually quite up to date as to what licenses and permits are needed in the different areas and cities of the United States.

Should your city not be listed, your local government's website should have the necessary information. It is only a few clicks away!

Two types

- Usually, though, a *general business license* is needed. Cities consider the renting of property as a business, and you are very likely to require a business license or permit to start renting out your property.

- Some cities delve deeper. They will require the entrepreneur to have a specific *short-term rental license* or permit. You can only get such a permit if your health and safety requirements are met, if you comply with zoning laws and if adjoining properties have been notified of your intentions.

In the Zone

We've touched on this already, but it is important enough to mention again.

It is imperative to make sure if any zoning laws apply to the area in which your rental unit lies.

There are no two ways about it: if your property falls within a restricted zone or an area where rentals are banned, you don't have many alternative options.

It is best to make sure of this before you spent money on getting your rental ready. In some cities, zoning rules are strictly enforced, and it won't be long before a curious neighbor notifies the authorities.

The Taxman will come knocking.

There is income tax and self-employment tax. There might be a short-term rental occupancy tax.

Keep the records!

Taxes are part of regulations, and to be a successful Airbnb entrepreneur, you must be informed as to which fees are to be paid.

You might also be eligible to claim certain tax deductions, and you should contact your tax advisor if you want to know more about this.

Conclusion

Newcomers to the party

Airbnb and other short-term rental platforms have only recently entered the tourism industry. It is a whole new way of urban tourism, of shared experiences and living 'as a local.'

The industry is still a melting pot of indecision and trial-and-error. The regulations that administrate the sector are still constantly changing and trying to find a stable stand on which to rest.

For now, dear Airbnb entrepreneur, rest assured that your city will continue to take steps to protect residential neighborhoods and possible guests to your establishment. It is good. We need regulations. Rules also protect you, the entrepreneur. Be sure to take the steps outlined here to build the most successful short-term rental business that you can. It is a start.

How can an Airbnb entrepreneur partner with a real estate agent to adapt to regulations?

It is happening in France

Airbnb has recently launched a sub-letting service in France, in partnership with the US real estate franchise, Century 21. With this, the platform is officially starting to cater for longer-term letting.

Airbnb hosts in Paris are now allowed to sublet out their homes for up to 120 days per year.

How it works

If you signed a contract with a Century 21 property, you are eligible to sub-let your accommodation. A set revenue share divides the rental income 70-23-7 (tenant, owner, real estate agency).

It is a win-win deal because the landlord is automatically part of the process and tenants can earn some extra money by using Airbnb. City officials will also now be in a much better position to supervise sub-letting – a headache in the past.

There is no reason why this model could not be duplicated elsewhere in the world.

Not mom-and-pop operations anymore

The professionals want in.

Airbnb might have started as the rental of open vacation homes or the renting out of an unused garage apartment, but statistics now show that professionals are increasingly hopping on the bandwagon.

In fact, it has been estimated that more than 60% of all recent Airbnb bookings were in apartments, condos and even working hotels.

The demand is already here.

Tenants are sub-letting anyway, with- or without the approval of their landlords.

The time is now ripe for landlords to stake their claim. Historically, long-term leases were the norm, but far more money can be made from shorter-term contracts. A model such as the one now being tested in Paris can benefit both tenants and owners.

A pro-active approach

Within the framework

Supporters of the French model in the US say that in allowing short-term rentals without restrictions, people will be able to lease out their apartments **within** the proper regulatory framework.

Residential buildings such as apartment buildings and condos that were previously restricted by zoning and homeowner association laws will be able to join the short-term rental industry, without having to do it undercover.

Condo owners, for example, are hampered because some do not use their properties year-round. In Miami, absentee owners or investors would be able to rent out units on a short-term basis. If partnerships with estate agencies can become the norm, it can create maximum flexibility for owners.

'Hospitality blended with residency.'

Some developers are now also leveraging on the short-term rental trend.

Pillow, a start-up in San Francisco, uses estate agents to control short-term rentals within a specific building. The estate agent ensures local regulatory fulfillment, insure against damages and share in the revenue.

Apartments that stood empty or are not yet sold can now be utilized in earning some revenue for its owner or the developer. During lease-up periods, units can be rented out, fully furnished.

One of the main perks for the Airbnb entrepreneur is that the real estate company will be able to deal with any rules or regulations that need to be adhered to.

The whole idea or concept is something in-between ordinary residential letting and Airbnb as we knew it up until now.

There is more to come.

It is a little late, but ...

The industry has been asking for this revolution in a way for years. Now, Airbnb and other short-term rental platforms have listened and realized that the 'if you can't beat them, join them' approach can be lucrative to the sector.

Airbnb has recently announced plans to let property manager and real estate agencies deal with the Airbnb platform directly. Estate agents will be able to manage bookings directly, receive payments and more.

We are a friendly building!

The 'Airbnb Friendly Buildings' program is another initiative to encourage revenue sharing between apartment owners and landlords.

According to the rules of this program, home sharing is allowed within the desired constraints of the building, if the building is enrolled in the program.

A home owner's association can add conditions to the standard building rules, and the percentage of profit sharing between hosts and owners are agreed upon.

How can a real estate agent help with my Airbnb listing?

Listing a home on Airbnb can be daunting.

With the industry increasingly being regulated, some homeowners might feel intimidated.

A real estate agent will do a lot to ease the fears of owners and help with the year-on-year growth of short-term rental platforms. Some owners will just be relieved that the administrative burden is off them.

A real estate agent can help an owner or a tenant:

- To follow common-ground etiquette rules that hosts must be compliant to. These rules don't come with penalties, but it can have a significant impact on the success of your hosting enterprise. For instance, canceling on guests is a big no-no.

- Adhere to safety-, zoning and health regulations

- Get the necessary permits and registrations

- Know for how long a property can be rented out. This differs from town to town and county to county. If you have it wrong, you can be fined.

- Help you navigate the rules of your apartment block or homeowner's association, if not taking the job totally out of your hands.

- Help you report your rental income for tax purposes and keep track of deductibles. The key is to document everything.

Conclusion

New beginnings

The Paris initiative could be the start of a whole new revolution in the short-term rental industry. The sector can now be increasingly utilized (and regulated) in ways that will benefit lessees *and* property owners.

You don't have to own a property to cash in on the short-term rental trend. Within the regulatory framework, it will now be possible to let someone *pay you* to 'housesit' while you are on vacation yourself, and that **with** your landlord's blessing.

It remains to be seen how this will play out in the US scenario, but one thing is for sure: there are big things on the horizon.

Municipalities to clearly define regulations

Introduction

Not state regulated

The enforcement of short-term rental regulations is currently (mostly) left to municipalities.

It makes sense, as local zoning issues and registration requirements are best handled at the local level. Today, around 3,000 US cities and counties each have more than 50 short term rental listings.

The industry is growing, and regulations are evolving with it. It should, therefore, be a priority for municipalities to help short term rental entrepreneurs by clearly defining what their rules and regulations are. The focus of this blog is how this could benefit entrepreneurs.

800 local governments

In a recent survey of 800 local governments, only 25% of municipalities had clear regulations in place. 16% were in the process of adopting new rules, 6% were unsure of what to do, and a whopping 53% had no rules.

It is apparent that most communities have yet to figure out how to handle the unexpected boom in the informal short-term rental industry.

Why rules?

Without rules, entrepreneurs are left to their own devices, and over the longer term, this can backfire when the local municipality **does** decide to climb on the bandwagon. By that time the short-term rental landscape can be fixed and cause a host of problems for the regulatory body.

Rules and regulations can only benefit all of the parties involved.

What should municipalities do?

   1. Understand the context of the community

Each county differs

In each community, values vary. For some, safety is a priority. For others the preservation of a neighborhood is important. Municipalities should be clear in what is essential in their particular city or county.

Municipalities should, therefore, get a sense first of what is going on in their area. The following questions can help.

- Exactly how many short-term rental listings are there in the municipal district?
- Are they concentrated around a specific area?
- What types of housing are on offer?
- Are there times of year when more bookings happen?
- What is the price range in listing prices?

Indirectly, municipalities should also research the total picture.

- Are there many houses to rent in the community overall?

- Are they affordable?
- What other lodging options are there?

Socio-economic demographics should also be kept in mind.

How can this help the short-term rental entrepreneur?

Rules and regulations that are crafted by keeping the context of the community in mind can help hosts to offer the best experience within their area and to be clear as to what they are allowed to do.

Should short term rentals be clustered around particular old-town tourist attractions, rules that **prohibit** short-stays in nearby apartment buildings would not be the best way to go.

If there is a **shortage** in **long-term** rental units for locals, municipalities can consider helping short term rental entrepreneurs by offering them the option of being able to rent out their flat for short stays – should they be the long-term tenant.

If safety is a community concern, police presence should be up to standard. The entrepreneur will be able to assure his tenants.

2. **What can we enforce?**

We are coming for you!

Municipalities must know what are within their capacity to do. What is the use of rules and regulations that can't be enforced?

The overall regulatory environment must be considered, as well as the use of current and new resources.

Would more money be made available to enforce rules? Is there enough staff available to do inspections, for instance, or are the police on board to impose noise restrictions?

How can this help the short-term rental entrepreneur?

Everybody likes to know the framework of what is allowed and what not. The short-term rental entrepreneur would want to know that his municipality will rise to the occasion and enforce their own rules.

Rules and regulations that cannot be enforced or are not checked up upon will only lead to unnecessary frustration for the already busy entrepreneur and can lead to a lack of concern to adhere to rules over the longer term.

3. Clear definitions

Who can, and where?

Municipalities should clearly state who is allowed to host. They should indicate which type of housing units are allowed to be utilized as short-term rental units.

How can this help the short-term rental entrepreneur?

This is important for the short-term rental entrepreneur so that there will be no future questions about what qualifies as a short-term rental unit.

Airbnb listings can vary between camping in someone's backyard to the rental of a full house!

One can imagine a host's frustration if he finds out his newly decorated RV is not allowed to be rented out and that due to unclear municipal regulations.

4. Land use and zoning

Municipalities should know what their long-term plans are for certain areas in the community.

- Do they want to preserve a neighborhood? Then they should not allow too many listings within the region.

- Are there not many rental units available to locals? Harsher controls should be implemented so that available units are not all converted to short term rentals.

How can this help the short-term rental entrepreneur?

Unfortunately, prioritizing land use and zoning means that tradeoffs are inevitable.

The objective of a quiet neighborhood for residents might mean that short term rentals are only allowed near busy streets. This precludes homeowners and entrepreneurs from earning extra income.

On the other hand, the resourceful entrepreneur with the unit in the busy street can be an advantage to local businesses and restaurants **and** boost his own ratings.

Conclusion

Effective short-term rental regulation is a sticky issue.

There are no hard and fast rules. Every municipality or county should analyze its local context and needs before an efficient system can be implemented.

Entrepreneurs could benefit greatly within the short-term rental industry. If you know what you can and cannot do, the sky is the limit. However, municipalities do have a role to play to define regulations as clearly as possible and with the end-result in mind.

What is the result?

The ultimate result will be a happy entrepreneur balanced with a content neighborhood.

No matter what local issues there might be: if a municipality can be clear as to what their rules are and be willing to make changes where needed, the short-term rental industry boom can be beneficial to all of the parties involved.

What can municipalities do to get hosts to comply with regulations?

Host compliance in the short-term rental industry

Introduction

The winds of change

Jimmy Dean, the American actor, once said: "I can't change the direction of the wind, but I can adjust my sails always to reach my destination."

The short-term rental phenomenon has taken the world by storm.

Airbnb is currently valued at more than $31 billion. 25% of leisure travelers are now expected to stay in an Airbnb unit at least once. Other sites like VRBO, FlipKey and HomeAway are also gaining force.

Municipalities have been caught unaware, and many cities are under pressure to find the best way to balance the benefits of home-sharing for short term rental hosts with possible adverse effects that it can have in communities.

The strong 'wind' of the short-term rental industry is here to stay. The big challenge for municipalities lies in 'the adjusting of the sails' to reach their destination.

Why regulate?

There are five main reasons why municipalities want to regulate the short-term rental industry.

1. Hosting must be safe.
2. Possible tax revenue that can be gained.
3. Help permanent residents to keep on having affordable housing options.
4. The preservation of neighborhood character.
5. Other hospitality units such as hotels and B&B's are subjected to taxes, inspections, and compliance to health and safety codes. The short-term rental industry should be, too.

The reality for municipalities

The host must 'help.'

Unfortunately, most municipalities don't have unlimited resources to enforce short term rental rules and regulations effectively. It would be virtually impossible for a municipality employee (or even four of them in one office) to regulate the industry in a city manually. New listings are popping up daily.

One of the cornerstones of successfully implementing host compliance to municipality regulations is, therefore, voluntary self-registration.

The beauty of permits

A permit provides a mechanism through which short term rental owners can comply with regulations.

If this is a requirement, and the process is free and easy, municipalities can use the permitting process as a way to **implement** regulations such as the ban on short term rentals in certain areas.

Permits will also give the municipality a picture of the total short-term rental activity in the areas. It will identify hosts and won't leave the city to guess how many operators there are.

No red tape

It is vital that the bureaucratic red tape is not plastered all over permits. If so, short term rental owners would rather risk a fine than go through a lengthy process.

An easy way to identify honest hosts will be for the city to require all hosts to display their permit number prominently in their online advertisement. The placement of an ad without a number can be sufficient grounds for prosecution and further follow-up by the city.

Further issues in self-registration

Self-registration would rely on the short-term rental owners' **awareness** of new rules, how **easy** registration is, and what the perceived likelihood is of being **sanctioned** if not complying with the laws.

Proposed strategies

This article looks at strategies of how voluntary compliance can be increased among short term rental hosts. Thus, said in another way, what can municipalities do to get hosts to comply with regulations?

Three broad categories are identified: Education, partnerships with STR platforms and the use of the city's existing mechanisms.

1. Educate the public.

Partnerships needed

Hosts cannot comply with new regulations if they are unaware of them.

Municipalities need to partner with STR platforms and other STR organizations so that hosts can be informed of regulatory changes and existing rules. Most STR platforms such as Airbnb (and others) are willing to take the initiative to coordinate with city officials and notify residents.

Airbnb already has an extensive catalog of different US cities and outlines rules and regulations that apply in each county. It is likely that most short-term rental homeowners will first look there for information.

'Hey, it's a room in my house.'

Some hosts don't see themselves as actual business owners, and therefore they don't acquire permits. Violations might be unintentional. Most hosts would willingly register, especially if the process is free and easy. But, education would be needed.

A Public campaign

Municipalities can consider a broad public campaign to raise awareness as to what legal home sharing is and how it is defined within the particular county. The drive can outline how permits can be obtained and what fines are applicable for non-compliance.

Also, neighbors can be made aware of illegal short-term rentals in their community and how they can complain about it. Indirectly, this will help the city to identify non-permit holders and do something about them.

2. Partnerships with STR platforms

Special agreements with STR platforms

Municipalities could benefit if they seek individual agreements with short term rental platforms. It won't help to enforce just legal go-ahead, but solutions can also be found outside the dictatorial process.

If agreements between the city and platforms can be reached that is mutually beneficial to all – why not? It also has the advantage that the municipality is demonstrating its commitment to innovation and technological progress.

Possible ideas include:

- *Short term rental platforms can collect occupancy tax directly from a host transaction and pay it over to the city.*

Interestingly, if Airbnb helped the city of Los Angeles in 2015 (which it didn't) to collect occupancy tax on **every** booking, the lump sum payment to the municipality would have been $28,585,395.

Hosts are now seeking out STR platforms that offer this service. It is much easier for them if they don't have to calculate and pay over their tax. As a result, Airbnb now actively pursue lump sum agreements with municipalities willing to engage in the process.

- *The permit application can be made part of signing up to an STR platform.*

Municipalities can negotiate with STR platforms to incorporate an option (in the signing-up process) for hosts to authorize STR platforms to collect and send host information to the city for permit processing.

A tick-box will be the fastest and most comfortable. A warning can be added that tells hosts that a valid permit number is essential to them operating their business.

If they choose not to tick the box, they must know that their information will also be forwarded to the municipality's STR permitting department.

There would be costs to the municipality:

- o   A system would be needed to receive the permit data from the STR platform.

- o   Operating such a system will result in administrative costs, as a more significant number of applications needs to be processed.

- o   The back and forth process as the city verifies the information needed to confirm compliance will also increase costs.

However, in the end, the city will gain in the form of a much higher permit application rate.

- *STR platforms can work with the city to remove egregious violators' online ads.*

Airbnb is already interested in doing this and municipalities have had success in asking Airbnb to remove individual ads of 'bad penny' hosts.

Some rental hosts turn entire buildings into rental units or operate many STR units across a city. Some defy noise ordinances.

Airbnb complies and helps municipalities because they are concerned about their total image. Such voluntary agreements between the city and STR platforms can speed up the removal of bad actors and benefit the whole industry.

3. Use the city's current enforcement mechanisms.

'You will get caught.'

Research shows that a majority of people will adhere to the law if they think there is a high probability that they will be caught out if they do not.

However, seen realistically, municipalities do not have any funds available for enforcement across the board to prosecute every non-compliant host. The cost and effort would be enormous.

Create the perception

It is attainable, however, to create an environment that reduces motivation for hosts to commit violations. Municipalities can seek out the most egregious violators by monitoring them online and by letting police officers respond to continuous neighborhood complaints.

- *Online monitoring is daunting.*

    In Los Angeles, the active Airbnb listings in 2015 that did not meet the city's definition of a primary residence were almost 5,000.

    It would be impossible to follow up on all of them. Therefore, municipalities should focus on areas where the public sees the problem as the most acute. They should also make sure that – if they follow up on a name and address – that the perpetrator will be revealed.

    The purpose of this strategy is to make the best use of the city's time and create the 'perception' that the city is on to violators.

- *Neighborhood complaints*

    Municipalities can utilize neighborhood complaints as a method to identify short term rental operators in defiance of rules.

    The advantages are:

    o   The city can match actual addresses to online advertisements.

    o   Operators that can cause harm to neighborhoods through disruptive behavior can be identified. Municipalities should give such hosts not more than three chances before revoking their permits.

    o   A functioning complaint system increases the perceived probability of being sanctioned, which is part of the whole plan.

Technology can help

For municipalities to effectively implement short-term rental regulation, some level of resources should be invested in compliance monitoring and enforcement.

However, most local governments are not technically equipped to do this themselves.

Why?

- The short-term rental industry is vast. New sites are popping up all the time.

- Manual monitoring (as mentioned before) is virtually impossible without a sophisticated database. Properties are added continuously, removed and changed.

- Address data is hidden on home-sharing websites. It is almost impossible to identify individual properties or owners based just on the information available when accessing the sites.

- Currently, listing websites do not enforce the listing of a permit number together with an advertisement. 'Illegal' properties can therefore not be identified.

- It is impossible to manually calculate how often properties are rented out and for how much. Municipalities, therefore, don't know the amount of taxes owed by any individual property owner.

A gap in the market

Luckily, new innovative companies have popped up so that municipalities can now effectively outsource the technology needed to help them achieve their goals.

Companies such as Host Compliance have developed 'big data technology' and have succeeded to bring compliance monitoring costs down to a minimum.

It is now possible for municipalities to outsource all the work associated with the enforcement of STR regulation in return for a percentage of the fees, tax- and fine revenues that these companies help collect. There is no need to utilize internal staff. No up-front investment or complex IT integration is needed. It is a win-win situation for all.

These companies manage registration, address identification, tax collection, permitting and complaint processes. Municipality staff can focus on their other normal day-to-day activities.

Conclusion

There is no doubt about it – the whole hot issue around regulation and host compliance is a valid one. Self-regulation, as opposed to government-imposed regulations, is preferable.

There is a lot that municipalities can do:

- They can educate short term rental hosts to be responsible
- They can partner with STR platforms to create win-win situations
- They can use their own enforcement resources, and/or they can partner with innovative new technology companies to help them.

STR's are not unwilling to help municipalities

To date, short term rental platforms had been very willing to comply with municipalities and the challenges they face. They use their financial and technological resources to help districts achieve their goals.

Of course, local governments must also be willing to rethink existing strategies so that home-sharing services can operate freely.

Let's go with the new revolution.

In the past, innovations had been disregarded just because people don't understand them. This should not be the case here. Change has already begun. The new era is here.

Larger cities and municipalities are embracing the STR concept and are building upon it with bike-sharing programs, and more.

Municipalities would be wise to encourage growth and development. If not, they would miss out on the next grand economic upheaval.

Airbnb Regulations in Los Angeles, CA

Introduction

In this series, we are looking at different US municipalities and how they apply rules and regulations within their counties. Can you, as an Airbnb entrepreneur, succeed there? What should you look out for?

Los Angeles

In our first case study, we put Los Angeles in California, under the microscope.

Now, on the website

At the moment, on the Airbnb website, the following is required from a new Airbnb host:

- A business license
- The review of zoning laws – the host should review what type of establishment applies to him.
- A 14% transient occupancy tax charged by the City of Los Angeles on the listing price for stays 30 days or less. Airbnb collects this tax and remits it to the City.

Short term rentals in Los Angeles up to now meant 'a portion of a residential building' that is used for fewer than 30 days per year.

Overall, short term rentals are prohibited in the city, except through a Conditional use permit.

However, Los Angeles is a top destination for travelers. Its municipality has been forced to look at its zoning regulations and face the problem of the already limited housing stock within the city.

Developments

Up until now, the city of Los Angeles had a very loose regulatory structure. It was impossible to distinguish if hosts only shared their homes on occasion and if they converted full houses to hotels.

The city lost thousands of potential homes to the short-term rental industry and thus contributed to homelessness. Also, due to the lack of rules, it has become tough for locals to get rental units at affordable prices within the city.

A new ordinance has been proposed. Now, the city wants to really define short term rentals and the types that will be permitted.

The idea is to curb negative impacts on neighborhoods and housing stock and provide a legal framework for responsible home sharing.

Recent changes in Airbnb rules

In December 2018, the city council of Los Angeles voted in a new regulation for the short-term rental industry. The new law is supposed to go into effect in July 2019.

No hosting in secondary properties

This law allows citizens to only host rentals from their primary residence – therefore, they must be residing there. Consequently, the host will not be permitted to operate a short-term rental unit from a second home or an investment property anymore.

Three years in the making

This proposal has been coming along for three years as councilmen argued that city homes could not be utilized as 'hotels.'

It is, of course, much more profitable for landlords to instead rent out their units on short term rental platforms than to tenants of lesser means. In the end, a vast housing crisis has developed.

Rules at the moment

As it stands, at the moment, hosts are barred from renting out a home for fewer than 30 days within the city. However, the rules have not been enforced, and some operators even won when confronted by the municipality.

The new rules

The new rules state that short term rentals can only be operated within a residence when hosts reside for at least half of the year.

Hosts need to register with the municipality, keep records, pay taxes and more. The cap is short stays of up to 120 days annually. If you hired out a granny flat and registered it with an STR platform before the 1st of January 2017, you will be allowed to keep on doing so.

Without registering, you will not be able to list your rental on any platform.

The cap can be exceeded

If hosts can prove that they are abiding to the rules or that their unit will not hurt the neighborhood, they can offer up space in their homes from more than the prescript 120 annual days. They must state their case to planning officials.

However, the extension to year-round hosting will not be granted if the host has any nuisance violation against him.

Off-limits

Apartments covered by the 'Rent Stabilization Ordinance' or affordable housing covenant units are not eligible to be rented out by their owners. This will protect renters.

How will the new rules be enforced?

Short term rental units are now to be registered. Home sharing units without valid registration numbers will be issued with a notice of violation and fined if they don't stop their activities.

The Administrative Citation Enforcement (ACE) and Administrative Nuisance Abatement (ANA) programs will be used as enforcement tools.

New requirements on the hosting platforms

Short term rental platforms such as Airbnb or HomeAway are now, according to the new rules, not allowed to process bookings from unregistered hosts or hosts who rented out their homes for more days than permitted annually. Fines of up to $1,000 *per day* can be imposed on the platforms themselves.

The city now also asks for host information to help them with the enforcement of the rules.

Airbnb is not keen to supply this but would be open to forward registered hosts in the city to the municipality if vacation rentals (from secondary homes or investment property) could be allowed in L.A. HomeAway argues that some travelers are looking for these options and it must be given to them.

Tweaks are possible

The new regulations will most likely be reviewed in six months or a year.

Vacation rentals considered?

The new rules are set to go into effect in July, but the legalization of pure vacation rentals is still an open debate. It might be allowed in the future but capped in number. Some exceptions on rent-stabilized apartments may also be considered.

Protect and preserve

The proposed changes in the short-term rental industry in Los Angeles have the job to protect rental housing and to preserve neighborhoods. The city council stated that they were looking out for people who were genuinely trying to make ends meet by hiring out their personal property.

Success?

In the end, the success will boil down to how effectively the regulation of the home-sharing industry can be enforced. The city of Los Angeles does not have an excellent track record of administrative rule enforcement.

Conclusion

The STR entrepreneur in Los Angeles

The purpose of this article was to review how favorable the short-term rental industry in Los Angeles is in terms of rules and regulations to you, the STR entrepreneur.

It seems that, due to the new ordinances, only a primary house owner will be able to reap the rewards of renting out a home sharing unit after July 2019.

Will I get away with not meeting the terms?

Operating under the radar could be a possibility if you are dishonest and in lieu of a registration number, but it is expected that after three years of drafting, the city will be adamant in at least trying to enforce their new ordinances.

Overall, the STR platforms are not unwilling to co-operate with municipalities. It can be expected, that although the going might be tough in the beginning, a more streamlined process will be incorporated in time to ensure that host registration and host information will be shared between the city and the STR platforms. It will become easier to identify rogue hotel operators and fine them.

As stated, pure vacation rentals and the sharing of rent-stabilized units may become possible in the future.

It remains to be seen how the situation will play out, but after July 2019, you must be a homeowner with a registration number to be successful in-home sharing in Los Angeles.

Airbnb Regulations in Paris, France

Introduction

In the second of our series on Airbnb municipalities and how they apply regulations, we look at France, and then, in particular, Paris.

There is no doubt about it: France is a prime destination, and the growth of Airbnb has also spurred on the phenomenal growth in the short-term rental industry in its cities.

It is understandable, then, that municipal regulation here is necessary and a hot topic.

STR is not allowed everywhere in France

A new host must first make sure that hosting on a particular property is allowable. France has quite a lot of restrictions, accommodation categories, and specific regulatory obligations.

The money you earn through Airbnb in France is considered taxable, and you should be aware of the different rules and how it is relevant to you and your establishment.

Then, there are specific rules that only apply to Paris. We will be addressing that.

General rules and regulations for STR in France

The French Association of Short-Term Rentals and Airbnb made voluntary commitments to the French government in 2018 to show their support of healthy tourism in France. As a result, three listing categories for the industry were devised.

A primary residence

A primary residence for short term rental purposes in France is considered the place where you live for at least 8 months per year. The host is allowed to rent out the full house/unit for 120 days per year.

A room in a primary residence has no imposed limits on it. It can be rented out throughout the year. It need not be declared to the city.

A secondary residence

If you live somewhere in France for less than four months per year (as in a holiday home), it can be rented out 365 days per year, provided that you declare it to the city. Some large cities will require you to file a 'change of use' to get permission to rent out your secondary residence.

Hotels, apartments, and bed and breakfasts.

The last listing category for the short-term rental industry in France is non-residential spaces, or alternatively, housing spaces for tourists. Hotels, serviced apartments and B & B's all fall in this grouping.

STR rental taxes in France

Host income to be automatically reported in 2020

Recently a law has been passed in France where STR platforms such as Airbnb are required to provide tax authorities with annual gross income and number of transactions.

This will come into effect in January 2020 and is automatic between the platforms and French Tax Authorities.

Some more tax issues:

- *Hosts* must report income from STR on their annual tax returns. Airbnb helps with this by sending hosts their annual earnings statement each year in January.

- Residential or property taxes are payable depending on whether you are a tenant or owner.

- Furnished rentals are not subject to VAT.

- France has the micro-BIC declaration of earnings. If you fall within an annual revenue limit, you are eligible for flat-rate tax discounts. For example, for furnished residential premises, the flat-rate can be 50% off your income if your income did not exceed €70,000 in two years.

  The threshold for this scheme is raised to €170,000 for ranked tourist accommodation and a 71% reduction in taxable income if you earn less than the stated amount in one year.

- Income can be exempted from tax if you ask a reasonable rent price and your earnings did not exceed €760 per year.

- Professional bed and breakfasts are treated differently. These establishments are liable for VAT and property rental tax. They also report under different reporting systems and can fall under the para-hotel tax system.

- From July 2018, Airbnb collects **tourist tax** on the host's behalf and send it to the respective city administration.

Tax issues are confusing in France! It is difficult even for French people to understand everything.

Airbnb hosting in Paris, France

When in Paris

From October 2017, owners of primary- and secondary residences in Paris are required to get a registration number from the Paris City hall before they are permitted to host guests. Individual rooms and long-term rentals (more than three months) need not be registered.

In Paris, only owners can rent out their units.

Subletting is mostly forbidden. A renter may sub-let with **written permission** from the owner but is only allowed to make up to the rental amount that is to be paid to the owner.

This is useful if the renter goes on holiday. He can then guarantee his rent to the owner but is not allowed to make additional money off the unit.

Tit for tat

Also, STR rules in Paris require you to purchase an equivalent surface of long-term rental space, should you transform an existing residential space into a short-term unit. This is called 'compensation.'

The idea behind it is that when you short term rents a house to tourists, residents can't rent it over the longer term and the city should be 'compensated' for it. The additional unit you provide can then be utilized.

It might look as if the cost is too high, but it is all in the ratios. Holiday letting (or short-term rental) in Paris, can enable hosts to generate rental income of *more than double on average* rental.

It might therefore not be such a bad idea to consider getting that additional long-term rental unit, if it enables you to generate a more significant income over the long run off your STR property and especially if your property has a good potential for holiday letting.

The illegal rentals problem in Paris

Unregistered rentals

In Paris, there is currently a massive problem with illegal rentals. According to the city, the rules are not enforced forcibly enough from the Airbnb's side.

Businesses are not registered and don't display their registration number on adverts. There are hundreds of illegal rentals on the site, and the city of Paris is suing Airbnb for €12.5m

'A museum city.'

Some city officials mean that Paris is being made into a 'museum city,' reserved exclusively for tourists. Residential housing is turned into tourist destinations, and the locals suffer from it.

Airbnb is accused of breaking the law by listing almost 1000 homes that are not officially registered with the city – and that while registration became compulsory already in December 2017.

The registration system was designed to ensure that properties are not rented out for more than the allowed 120 days per year and to ensure that people pay their taxes.

But, homeowners are not adhering to the rules. The city of Paris wants to hold Airbnb accountable – and according to the law, this means a fine of €12,500 for each unlawful listing.

Paris is one of Airbnb's top markets with more than 65 000 short term rentals advertised on that platform alone. As a result, locals and hospitality experts feel that holiday rentals are fueling home speculation and it is becoming impossible to buy property in the city. Paris is the process of being lost to the locals.

Airbnb is opposing the allegations and is saying that they are adhering to the rules and that they are in the process of getting hosts to comply.

Conclusion

The STR entrepreneur in France

A foreigner in France

Rules and regulations in France are not always easy to understand. It may be well worth your while to get some expert consultation – especially if you are a foreigner wanting to invest in a France short term rental unit.

There are much more to the tax issues that are listed here, and a specialist can give you the best advice.

Will I get away with not meeting the terms?

Our stance on the issue is: No. The city of Paris is already up in arms about preserving their local neighborhood, and one can expect that the issue will become more heated.

The best policy would be to carefully research what rules and regulations apply to your establishment, get some advice on tax issues and stick to it.

Airbnb Regulations in Toronto, Canada

Introduction

The New York of Canada

Oh, Toronto! It is a cosmopolitan, large city with an exciting vibe.

Toronto is the most visited city in Canada, and with its multi-cultural heritage, it is often called the 'New York' of Canada. The sprawling city has much to offer visitors, and it is no wonder that it is not an easy feat to regulate the STR industry in this city.

This article examines the short-term rental industry in Toronto and the recent new rules that were proposed to regulate it.

Home draining in Toronto

A recent report states that Airbnb alone 'took' more than 6,000 homes out of the loop for locals in Toronto. Families are seeking homes and can't find it.

New regulations in December 2017

New rules were passed by the Toronto City council in December 2017 but can currently not be enforced due to a hanging appeal. The appeal will only be heard in August 2019.

What happened?

The new restrictions on Airbnb were set to go into effect this June, but three short-term rental operators appealed to this bylaw change.

No new regulations can be enforced until the appeal is heard and the city of Toronto is losing out on an estimated $1,000,000 in operating and charging fees.

The main problem is the fact that the Local Planning Appeal Tribunal replaced the 'old' Ontario Municipal Board – as 'faster, fairer and more affordable' service. However, the new tribunal has a backlog of old cases filed under the OMB; for this reason, the extended lead time.

What can happen?

Should the new rules be enforced immediately, more than 8,000 homes on Airbnb will have to be removed as they are not in compliance with regulations. (About 65% of listings on Airbnb in Toronto are for entire homes.)

It can place homes back into the long-term housing market and give relief to thousands of families seeking permanent residence.

Airbnb's retort

Airbnb says that they are not trying to avoid regulation. In fact, they advocate for fair, sensible home sharing regulations. They say the report as mentioned above was based on faulty assumptions and that they **want** to be regulated.

The December 2017 new licensing regulations

Should the new regulations come into effect, the following are the rules that the STR industry would have to abide by.

1. **It is for STR**

The regulations are for short term rentals.

Short term rentals here are defined as all rental units that are rented out for *less* than 28 consecutive days. All rental bookings for less than 28 days, therefore, have to stomach the new rules, whereas more extended stays are exempted.

Up to three rooms allowed.

Up to three rooms within a house can be rented out (for less than 28 days each.)

What about granny flats?

However, a suite or an apartment within a home does not fall under this rule. If there is an own entrance, a fridge or a stove involved, you can only rent out that unit for longer than 28 days at a time.

The only exemption is if the unit is that of a tenant and he is listing it himself. The tenant must be the primary resident of the unit.

2. **The 180 days rule**

STR hosts are allowed to rent out their units for a maximum of 180 days per year in total, no more.

3. **You must be the owner of the residence.**

The new licensing regulations ask for an STR host to be the owner of the unit he/she is renting out.

Also, no more than one unit can be registered to one person. In practical terms, this means that if you have a second property, you would not be allowed to rent it out for short periods.

$50 registration fee

An annual registration fee of $50 is payable. A host can be fined up to $100, 000 if he is not registered. All operators will be paying the same amount, no matter how popular their unit is or how much it is rented out.

A registration number must be used when advertising on Airbnb and other STR platforms. No registration is needed for long term landlords.

4. **Privacy rules**

The city will own the registry of all of these STR owners. Operators in the STR industry will connect to the system through their platforms.

This means that the city of Toronto will have direct access to Airbnb host information, which will make enforcement of the rules much more manageable. It is not yet clear how the information will be used by the city and for how long.

How would the new rules be enforced?

'Enforcement rules.'

- When registering, new STR operators will have to provide the city with the number of nights their homes were rented out over the previous year.

- Companies will be required to keep detailed records for three years outlining identifying details of the owners, the number of nights each unit was rented out, the rental type and more.

- Should anyone complain about a unit in Toronto, an investigation will be launched and the owner fined if non-compliance to any rule is found.

- Two or more noise-, waste collection-, fire- and building code violations in the previous three years can disallow a host from registering his property.

Enforced by whom?

The city is still to make it clear exactly how they will enforce rules. By-law officers are most probably going to be in charge. Fines are set up by region and can be up to $100, 000 for non-compliance.

Company rules

Website based companies

Online Airbnb-like companies offering facilitating services between a renter and home operators will have to pay $5,000 for a municipal business license in Toronto. A further $1 per night per transaction will also be charged as an annual fee.

These companies would also be required to keep track of their hosts and see that they have valid registration numbers on STR platforms. They also have to set procedures in place to help counter neighborhood nuisances such as noise.

Others

Other companies that use conventional means to reach hosts and renters, such as real estate brokers, will not need this license.

It is still unclear how the city is going to distinguish between the two. It is possible that loopholes around this regulation are going to surface.

Why the difference?

The most likely answer is the fact that the city of Toronto and its policymakers want to make it difficult for online operators to grab a share of the market and therefore take more units out of the long-term picture. It is, after all, much easier for them.

Brick and mortar companies, such as real estate companies, have other focuses of interest and will not have such a significant effect on the total STR industry.

The STR rentalpreneur in Toronto

More houses for locals

One can see from the proposed new rules that it is aimed at decreasing the housing shortage in Toronto.

Second homes, for instance, can no longer be utilized as STR units but can be opened up to the hundreds of people waiting to rent a home in the city on a long-term basis. The regulators are hoping that this will happen.

A blanket ban

The most sweeping potential change in the STR industry in Toronto is that fact that you can't rent out your home if you can't prove that you are not the prime owner. You can only get a license to operate if you can demonstrate that you meet the city's requirements.

Yes, it might be possible to use some friends and family as fronts, but large operators with several units would probably need to turn to the long-term rental market if they want to survive and make an income from their real estate.

This is precisely the aim of the new proposed licensing requirements: short term rentals do have a place in the city, but the dire housing situation must be addressed.

'I am a company'

The new propose harsher rules to keep online companies in check will probably have a significant effect on the short-term rental industry in Toronto as soon as it comes to pass. Only the huge players will be able to survive the enormous licensing fees.

Conclusion

No new rules yet

Currently, the new rules are not yet in place because of the hanging appeal. It remains to be seen what is going to happen after August 2019 and how (and if) the new rules and regulations will be implemented.

What is true, though, is that the landscape of the STR industry is set to change in Toronto in a big way. Operators who had the last year to still make some money off their second homes or apartments are most likely going to be impacted.

Airbnb Regulations in Australia

Introduction

We are on our fourth blog that discusses different rules and regulations for short term rentals in different parts of the world and how it may affect you, the rentalpreneur.

For this blog, we travel all the way 'Down Under.' How does the STR industry look in Australia?

An overview

- There were an estimated 180, 000 Airbnb listings in Australia in 2017.
- Homes available for rent jumped from just under 44, 000 in 2016 to almost 90, 000 in 2017.
- A lot of users are listing more than one unit.
- Host earnings increased with over 60% in 2017 from 2016.

There is no doubt about it. The industry has been welcomed and adopted massively. Accountability and regulations is a definite need.

Strata schemes

It is an Australian innovation in property law.

Strata title allows individuals to own part of a property (called a 'lot,' but it is actually an apartment or a townhouse) while having them share common property (foyers, driveways, and gardens).

All are governed by a legal entity – a body corporate if you like. It all began about 50 years ago and is now extremely popular in Australia.

How many are there?

It is estimated that there are more than 2.6 million strata 'lots' in Australia with an insured value of $995 billion. In Sydney alone, it is estimated that strata account for more than half of all residential sales and leases.

Strata plan developments can include residential units, commercial units, retail units, and even caravan parks and resorts. There are even strata-titled vineyards in Western Australia!

Airbnb in Stratas

At the moment, it is unclear how legal Airbnb is operating within strata schemes – it all depends on individual strata schemes and how their body corporate works.

Some schemes banned STR units entirely due to damage to communal property, increased costs and health and safety risks.

New legislation 2018

In June 2018, the **New South Wales** government accepted new regulations that will impact the STR industry in a big way.

Up to that date, land use in NSW was regulated by an act that required councils to prepare LEP's (Local Environment Plans.) It controlled hotels, and B & B's, but STR services came to overthrow the apple cart.

Short-term stays were more challenging to regulate than the other types of accommodation.

The new policy has the following rules:

1. **The Body Corporate or Strata Owners Corporation can decide**

They can decide if they want to ban STR stays totally, or not. The Body Corporate will have the banning power in a building if:

- The owner of the lot is not living in the unit
- if 75% of owners agree to pass the bylaw to ban STR's

Conversely, if an owner is living in his unit and only wants to rent out a room for a few nights per year (perhaps while he is away), he may do so, except if the **majority** of owners in a building say that they don't want holiday letting to occur in their building.

This regulation targets investors who are only buying apartments to list on STR platforms or tenants who sublet without their landlord knowing.

2. **180 days per year**

Hosts can let out their homes for up to 180 days per year. This roughly matches up with the number of weekends, school- and public holidays per year.

3. **A code of conduct**

Short-stay operators must agree to sign up to a code of conduct. It is mandatory, and it will address issues such as damage to the property, noise, and disruptive guests.

Two serious breaches within two years will mean that a guest or a host will be banned from the STR industry for five years. Individuals can also be fined up to $220, 000 and businesses to $1.1 million.

4. Enforcement

The NSW Department of Fair Trading will be tasked with enforcing the new rules. They will do this by:

- Appointing a panel to assess complaints
- Use data from STR platforms to review complaints
- Keeping watch over letting agents and STR online platforms
- Maintain a register of strikes against individuals and businesses

What would new regulations accomplish?

No more tourists hogging prime units

Housing will be more affordable for the locals. The new legislation hopes to help locals to find long-term rental units easier.

Who are you, again?

Disruptions in strata schemes will be minimized. As it is now, actual residents are faced with strangers sharing their pools, gyms or tennis courts without considering neighbors or long-term maintenance.

Less property damages

The new rules hope to counter the risk of out-of-control renters and property damage in strata.

There are some arguments *against* the new legislation.

- *It is not the law*

Some lawyers feel that merely updating bylaws in the Strata Living handbook (as the Department of Fair Trading did it) is not the law yet. For them to say that ordinances that restrict STR units are 'invalid' means nothing until the courts determine it.

This leaves significant loopholes for the rentrepreneur with an aggressive focus and a deep pocket. It is technically possible to do what you want in Australia's strata and have the law decide your case over the long term.

- *The rental market is actually not affected.*

    Researchers found that Airbnb actually represents less than 4% of the total Sydney rental market. When comparing median rent and its average annual increases, the research found no link between 'high' STR listings and rises in rent in Sydney.

    The only affected neighborhoods are those in high-socioeconomic areas that are tourist magnets.

- *It is counter-productive*

    Some feel that the new legislation will stifle innovation in the STR industry. Legislation can lead to a patchwork of regulations across Australia and drive up the cost of accommodation, curtailing the overall economic potential of the STR phenomenon.

It is still early days. Most owner corporations in strata are still unsure what the new laws would mean and how it will work in practice.

The STR industry in Western Australia

Airbnb and other STR platforms are arguing for minimal regulations in Western Australia.

During the past 12 months, $155 million were injected into the state's economy by almost 600, 000 Airbnb guests visiting Western Australia. These STR platforms share wealth with people that traditionally missed out.

Councils with different types of rules in Western Australia are hindering total growth, according to industry experts.

They are calling for a light touch in regulations for Western Australia as the region could benefit by more tourists. Tourists are not streaming to Western Australia because they *found the destination on Airbnb*, but rather *because* Airbnb is operating there.

The STR entrepreneur in Australia

So, how favorable is the short-term rental industry in Australia is in terms of rules and regulations to you, the STR entrepreneur?

The Council will have the final say.

In New South Wales, there are still some zoning restrictions in place. Councils have specific and different regulations for STRs.

Some require consent or development permits from the council; others say you are to provide meals. Currently, only 12 councils in NSW allow homeowners to lease their homes.

No restrictions in Victoria and Queensland

In Victoria and Queensland, owner corporations cannot restrict owners, and they can freely use STR platforms. However, should a guest damage common property, owners can be ordered to pay neighbor compensation.

Host protection insurance

Hosts in Australia are protected with insurance of up to $1 million, but it does not cover everything. Common property within strata is excluded, as well as physical harm to a guest while he is on your property.

Tax

Tax earnings in Australia must be declared. The Australian Tax office has stated that they will police current properties on STR platforms and will be auditing some of them.

On the positive side, the rentalpreneur can claim for expenses such as water, electricity, internet, phone use, and even repairs.

Conclusion

Fundamental regulations

For the most part, Australia is still in the desert when it comes to the management of the STR industry. Its legislators still have to catch up with worldwide trends.

Rules and regulations vary significantly from state to state, from council to council and from zone to zone.

Check up in your state, zone.

For now, the best way forward in Australia for STR entrepreneurs is to be very sure of the local council's rules and regulations and to make sure that you are protected by insurance.

Strata changes

Some owners are challenging the bylaws of their strata. Annoyed at being barred from a lucrative income, some take their cases to court.

However, there is a lack of uniformity in convictions as there are no clear-cut rules.

The new business model of sharing accommodation has changed the nature of the hospitality industry, and it is now clear that some or other cohesive policy for the STR industry are needed in Australia.

New South Wales to lead

The new rules and regulations in New South Wales will hopefully pave the way for a better-regulated industry in the years to come.

Airbnb Regulations in Israel

Introduction

In the last blog in our series of case studies for STR units, we go to Israel and specifically, it's West Bank.

Robust tourist community in Israel

In the whole of Israel, there are more than 20,000 hosts who have helped visitors to travel all over Israel to enjoy its cultural and religious heritage.

Tel Aviv alone has more than 8,000 apartments and rooms listed on Airbnb – almost equal in number than the number of hotel rooms. The city's occupancy rate for tourism bed nights in 2017 was 74%.

The Israeli-Palestinian conflict

The Israeli-Palestinian conflict is controversial, and it is one of the world's longest-running conflicts. At its heart, it is a conflict between two parties who wants the same territory, but it is much more complicated than only that fact.

The Airbnb position

Airbnb as a company is torn about what they should be doing in occupied territories that are the subject of historical disputes - such as the conflict between the Israelis and the Palestinians.

Some say no

Some say no, companies should not be able to profit in such areas.

Others say, why not? If people-to-people travel is the notion and if it can help bring people together, it has value.

International law

Airbnb is permitted by international law to engage in business in Israel. They hold the stance that they will listen to experts, ask questions, seek out the hosting and traveler's community for their thoughts and that they will continue to learn how to operate in occupied territories.

A framework

They have developed a framework of how to evaluate listings in occupied territories.

- They believe in a case-by-case approach and the recognition that every situation is unique.
- They consult with experts and community leaders
- Safety is paramount and they asses the risks continuously
- Are there listings that contribute to human suffering?
- Are there listings in an occupied territory that has a direct connection to a broader dispute?

Listings in the occupied West Bank

When applying this decision-making framework, Airbnb concluded in November 2018 that listings in the Israeli settlements in the occupied West Bank should be removed due to safety reasons.

They also felt that the mere allowance of the listings contribute to the suffering of inhabitants as a whole as it shines a light on it.

The idea was delisting about 200 properties.

The problem in a nutshell

There are about 400,000 Israeli settlers illegally living in the West Bank, a holdup to the creation of an independent Palestinian state. The Israeli's say that the territory is disputed and that the fate of the settlement is still up in the air.

A boycott movement

A Palestinian boycott movement called for sanctions against Israeli settlers, and in return, Israel has enacted a law banning foreigners that knowingly supports this from entering the country.

SodaStream, French construction company, Veolia and the mobile giant, Orange, was subsequently banned from operating in Israel.

The boycott movement is happy about Airbnb's decision to delist properties, but Human Watch Rights feel that Israel is prioritizing its support for the settlements above what is good for the country as a whole.

Israel has a thriving tourism industry and relies on the STR services industry. Sanctions could affect lodging and its cost in a negative way.

Settler hosts feel that they are part of Israel and unfairly discriminated against.

Tourism Boom

The delisting of the properties was announced just as Israel was expected to break records for inbound tourism.

More than 4 million tourists arrived in the country in 2017. Critics to the decision said that only Israelis were targeted and Palestinians in the West Bank could operate as usual.

Tax requirements

Around the same time as the Airbnb announcement, the Israel Hotel Association began asking tax authorities in Israel to enforce statutory tax requirements in the STR industry. Their stance was that the current industry encouraged tax evasion and that hotels are coming second.

If a host rents out a unit for more than three months in total per year, a tax rate should be applied that is comparable to hotel tax. It can be four times higher than the regular fee.

The Hotel Association feels that Airbnb apartments are rented out over the longer term, damaging the quality of life for permanent residents. Rental-market prices are also on the rise. Tourist and long-term accommodation must reach more of equilibrium.

The motion was approved at the time, but it is still unsure when the new policy will take effect and by how much property tax will be increased.

Tax as retaliation?

In some articles on the subject, it is said that the higher taxes are not really necessary, but that it is rather a retaliation on Airbnb's decision to ban listings from the West Bank settlements.

The Israeli Tourism Minister called the maneuver a 'discriminatory decision,' and he said that Airbnb should not be allowed to make money in Israel. Hosts in the West Bank were encouraged to sue STR platform.

Airbnb's change of heart

Tourist first.

In April 2019, after five months, Airbnb had a change of heart. The company announced that it would permit properties in the West Bank to be listed permanently on the site. All and all, the listings were never entirely removed

Their official statement said that they want to keep striving to keep people together and help the tourism industry. All company profits from the West Bank will now also be donated to humanitarian aid organizations. The STR platform is planning to copy this approach in other parts of the world, too.

Encouraged by legal action?

It could be that Airbnb's change of heart was spurred on by twelve homeowners in the Israeli settlement that brought legal action in the United States against Airbnb. The twelve owners were dual citizens of both Israel and the US. The company's change in plans settled the case.

The primary thinking is that STR platforms are not allowed to refuse hosts based on their religious group or where they choose to live. It seems as if Airbnb has agreed. In a blog post, the company said that it had never tried to boycott Israel.

What does this mean, for you the STR entrepreneur?

A shift in platform use?

It is understandable that hosts in Jewish territory were very upset about the initial Airbnb decision. Not only were they blatantly boycotted by a platform that was supposed to be 'for the people by the people', but Airbnb also violated their own policy.

Airbnb's website says that discrimination would not be tolerated, yet they allowed it to happen. The fact that they adopted a "Disputed Regions policy" was not received well. It was not uniformly passed unto other disputed regions.

The STR entrepreneur in Israel and especially in the West Bank has reason to have lost faith in Airbnb.

With things patched up, however, it remains to be seen how strongly hosts will continue to hate Airbnb and shift to other STR platforms in protest.

Other regulations

Other rules and regulations are not yet well thought out for Israel as it is in other parts of the world. This researcher could find no concrete rules as to maximum days that the people of Israel are allowed to rent out their property or applicable zoning rules.

A rough 'three months per year' applicable to tax rules was the only reference that could be found as to maximum days that hosts are allowed to rent.

Conclusion

It seems as if the STR industry in Israel is still very much in its infant's shoes and it will be interesting to watch it progress (within the political climate and all of its dilemma's) over the years to come.

About the Author

MATT MALOUF

Matt Malouf is a Part Time Investor and Author with a degree in Engineering from USC. His daytime gig is in Traffic Management focusing on technology integration and his part-time business niche is International Real Estate Investing, and Writing.

Matt Malouf has always been fond of writing and helping people. Over a course of some time, he gained the strength and courage to finally pursue another one of his dreams which led him to writing his first book to share personal experiences with his readers. Matt aims to enlighten the path his readers walk on and to learn lessons from his mistakes.

Matt Malouf has introduced value engineering problem-solving techniques to help people achieve their life goals and walk in the wake of success. He is a motivated individual who yearns to expand the horizons of his knowledge.

= = = = = = =

CONTACT:

You can read and review more of Matt's work at:

http://amazon.com/author/mattmalouf

Matt can be reached and consulted through his Clarity account at:

https://clarity.fm/mattmalouf

http://twitter.com/mattbestselling

http://facebook.com/mattbestselling

Afterward

Thanks for coming to the end of our latest installment of Short-Term Rental Success Stories from the Edge, Volume 4: Beat the Regulations. We really diverted off our normal format with this one and felt this topic deserved a changeup, what did you think? Our next volume we will get back to more short and regular stories from our entrepreneurial friends around the world.

I envision this entire project to be eight volumes in total (this is volume four). If you would like to contribute, please reach out to me on my new Clarity page https://clarity.fm/mattmalouf or through my author page on Amazon and let's chat more! You can email me at matt@investwithmatt.com

We live in the sharing economy, and I believe we can help each other on our journey to short term rental success by doing just that: sharing our stories. What do you have to share? More than you think. Contact me and let's talk!

Upcoming "Stories from the Edge" will include expats moving overseas, investing in short term rentals, marketing your business, and something special....got suggestions? Email me and share! We hope you will join us!

www.ingramcontent.com/pod-product-compliance
Lightning Source LLC
Chambersburg PA
CBHW022128170526
45157CB00004B/1787